Powhatan, Native American Leader

by Susan Bachner

Boston, Massachusetts
Chandler, Arizona
Glenview, Illinois
Upper Saddle River, New Jersey

Illustrations
Opener, 1, 2, 3, 5, 9, 10, 11, 13, 14, 15 Graham Kennedy.

Photographs
Every effort has been made to secure permission and provide appropriate credit for photographic material. The publisher deeply regrets any omission and pledges to correct errors called to its attention in subsequent editions.

Unless otherwise acknowledged, all photographs are the property of Pearson Education, Inc.

Photo locators denoted as follows: Top (T), Center (C), Bottom (B), Left (L), Right (R), Background (Bkgd)

4 ©Visions of America, LLC/Alamy; 7 Library of Congress; 8 ©Ilene MacDonald/Alamy; 12 Library of Congress.

ISBN-13: 978-0-328-67687-3
ISBN-10: 0-328-67687-X

5 6 7 8 9 10 V0FL 16 15 14 13

Powhatan, a Powerful Leader

The year was 1607. A huge **lodge** rose on the banks of the York River in what is now Virginia. Inside stood the most powerful leader within hundreds of miles. He was tall and about 60 years old. Around his broad shoulders he wore a cape made of raccoon skins. Long chains of pearls hung around his neck. Surrounding him were many loyal fighters and servants.

This was no ordinary leader. This was Powhatan, who ruled over thousands of Native American people. Yet neither Powhatan nor his people knew that they would soon face major changes to their way of life. In fact, an entire continent was about to change. That spring, in 1607, the first **permanent** English settlers in the Americas were about to arrive.

A typical Powhatan village

Powhatan's Rise to Power

Powhatan was born in the 1540s. In all likelihood, his father ruled in what is now Florida, but Spanish settlers drove him and his people north. They settled in the area of modern Virginia. Here, Powhatan's father ruled over his own people as well as five other Native American groups. Together, they formed the Powhatan **Confederacy**.

When Powhatan became chief, he hoped to expand the confederacy and bring more Native American groups under his rule. His fighters were strong, smart, and courageous. They defeated many other Native American groups in the region. Some groups joined the confederacy out of fear. Others joined because they had married Powhatan people.

By 1607, the Powhatan Confederacy covered a large area of land. Powhatan is thought to have ruled over about 30 different Native American groups.

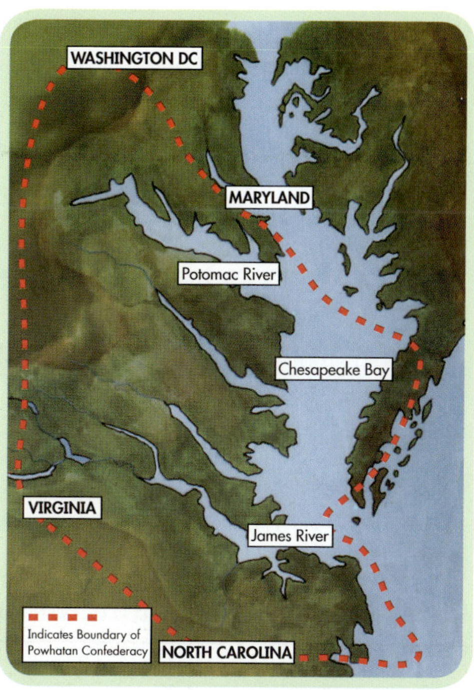

The Powhatan Confederacy is thought to have extended from what is today southern Maryland to northern North Carolina.

How Powhatan Ruled

As chief, Powhatan demanded gifts from the people under his rule. Every year, his subjects brought him animal skins, beads, and other valuable items. They also gave him corn, turkeys, deer, and other foods. These gifts served as symbols of Powhatan's power, but also helped support Powhatan's family. Powhatan also used them to reward his chiefs and to feed his fighters and servants.

How did Chief Powhatan hold his confederacy together? He replaced the chiefs of some groups with his own relatives. He also made sure that each group looked out for one another. In this way, his confederacy helped keep each group safe and ensured that each group remained loyal to him.

For many years, Powhatan was the supreme leader, and no one questioned him. That was about to change.

The English Arrive In Powhatan's Lands

In 1607, three ships from England sailed into Chesapeake Bay. These English ships were nothing like the dugout canoes used by the Powhatan people. However, these ships were familiar to the Powhatans. In years past, similar ships had sailed into the bay. Their crews had killed or kidnapped Native Americans.

On this day, the Powhatans watched a group of settlers row towards shore in small boats. The Powhatans forced the settlers to return to their ships. However, the English did not give up. Eventually, the settlers did make it to shore and build a fort. They chose a place that was not being used by the Powhatans at the time. It was on the James River, 60 miles inland from the mouth of Chesapeake Bay.

The English Settlers Meet Powhatan

A week later, some settlers took a boat up the river. When the settlers met Chief Powhatan, he was surrounded by his fighters and servants. The settlers were impressed by how Powhatan demonstrated **authority**. His people respected and feared him and Powhatan expected the English to do the same.

Hard Times for Jamestown

The Jamestown settlers were not prepared to survive in a wilderness. Many of the settlers were **gentlemen**. In England, they had paid other people to do work for them. In Jamestown, these men refused to do essential chores, such as planting seeds. As a result, the settlers began to run low on food soon after they arrived.

Chief Powhatan saw this as an opportunity. The English needed food and Powhatan wanted the metal weapons, tools, and bowls they had. Therefore, Powhatan offered to trade. Perhaps, he might even convince them to become part of his confederacy. With their support—and their weapons—Powhatan could attack his enemies and expand his great confederacy even more.

The English came for food and they agreed to trade their copper bowls for food. But they would not part with their weapons. They did not trust Powhatan and feared he would use the weapons against them. The relationship between the two groups began to change for the worse.

Investing in Jamestown

The Virginia Company in England paid for the ships and supplies needed to start the Jamestown colony. Investors gave money to the company, hoping to make money from the colony.

An Uneasy Peace

Late in 1607, John Smith became one of the leaders of Jamestown. When Smith set out to explore the area, Chief Powhatan's fighters captured Smith. They brought him back to the main village.

When Smith later recalled this event, he claimed that Powhatan sentenced him to death. Then, Smith said that Pocahontas, a young daughter of Powhatan, **intervened**. According to Smith, Pocahontas stopped her father from killing Smith.

Today, many historians do not entirely believe Smith's story. They think that Powhatan set up a **ceremony**, or ritual, to adopt Smith. By having Pocahontas save Smith from death, Powhatan intended to bring Smith into his confederacy.

Powhatan now viewed Smith as a member of his people. He let Smith go back to Jamestown. For the time being, there was peace between the two sides.

Pocahontas pleading for John Smith's life.

The English settlers built buildings in Jamestown that looked like English buildings.

The "Starving Time"

From 1608 to 1609, Smith ordered the English settlers to work hard. He did not want to have to depend on Powhatan. Still, it was Chief Powhatan who kept the settlers from going hungry. However, after two years, Powhatan grew tired of the English settlers' ongoing demands for food.

When John Smith returned to England in 1609, Powhatan planned a **siege** of Jamestown. He stopped providing food to the English. He kept a group of fighters near the fort. Whenever settlers came out of their fort, the Powhatans attacked them. The English could not hunt and many died from starvation.

Chief Powhatan's plan almost worked. However, in the spring of 1610, more settlers arrived from England. They brought plenty of supplies with them. Jamestown would survive, but would Powhatan's confederacy?

All-Out War

There were now more English settlers in the Powhatan people's homeland than ever before. The English began to take over land that the Powhatan people farmed. They also attacked several Powhatan villages. Once, they even destroyed an entire village and killed everyone, including children.

The English demanded more land and food. However, Chief Powhatan refused to give in to the English. Instead, his fighters attacked the settlers more often. During these attacks, Powhatan's fighters captured English weapons. As a result, the relationship between the two sides continued to grow even worse. Then, a single event changed everything. In 1613, an English captain decided to kidnap one of Powhatan's children.

The kidnapping of Pocahontas

Pocahontas, Powhatan's Favorite Daughter

Chief Powhatan had many children. But, according to John Smith, Pocahontas was by far Powhatan's "most dear and well-beloved." When she was young, Pocahontas had often visited Jamestown. Her father had sometimes sent her to deliver messages.

The result was that Pocahontas moved easily between the two cultures. She also knew that her father now saw the English as enemies. Yet, she was still curious about them—and fell right into the English captain's trap.

The English Kidnap Pocahontas

With the help of one of Pocahontas's friends, the English captain tricked Pocahontas into visiting his ship. Once on board, he prevented Pocahontas from leaving.

The English held Pocahontas for ransom. In exchange for her safe return, they wanted corn. They also demanded that Powhatan turn over all the weapons that he had captured. The English knew that having these weapons made Powhatan and his fighters stronger.

Chief Powhatan loved his daughter. At the same time, Powhatan realized that without the weapons, his people could not defend themselves against the English. He decided not to turn over the weapons. Instead, he claimed that they had been stolen or were broken and useless. However, the English did not believe Powhatan. They refused to let Pocahontas go and moved her from the ship to Jamestown.

In Jamestown, Pocahontas dressed in English clothes and learned how to speak English. Months in Jamestown turned into a year. Pocahontas was now living a new life.

Reluctantly, Powhatan refused to turn over weapons in exchange for his daughter.

A Second Attempt at Peace

While in Jamestown, Pocahontas met a settler named John Rolfe. Rolfe had discovered a type of tobacco that grew well in this region. He thought it could make a lot of money for the settlers. In 1614, the settlers shipped Rolfe's tobacco to England. Soon, many people in England wanted to buy this Virginia tobacco.

Pocahontas Marries John Rolfe

In time, Pocahontas and Rolfe became closer and decided to marry. When this news got back to Chief Powhatan, he gave his consent for them to marry. He sent a fine pearl necklace as a wedding gift to Pocahontas.

The English were happy about the marriage. Even though Powhatan knew his daughter was safe, he was sad because his daughter was giving up her way of life.

Before she married John Rolfe, Pocahontas converted to Christianity.

For a period of time, the marriage led to a new peace between Powhatan's people and the English. It was called the "Peace of Pocahontas."

The Trouble with Tobacco

Tobacco meant success for the Jamestown settlers. For the Powhatan people, tobacco meant more conflicts with the English. The settlers needed land to grow it, and they took over more and more of the Powhatan people's lands. As greater numbers of settlers poured into the Virginia colony to grow tobacco, Powhatan's people were forced to move farther inland. They had to leave the river valleys where they had farmed and fished for as long as they could remember.

Powhatan even moved his lodge and main village to get far away from the English. Powhatan said he wanted to "end my days in peace. . . laugh and be merry."

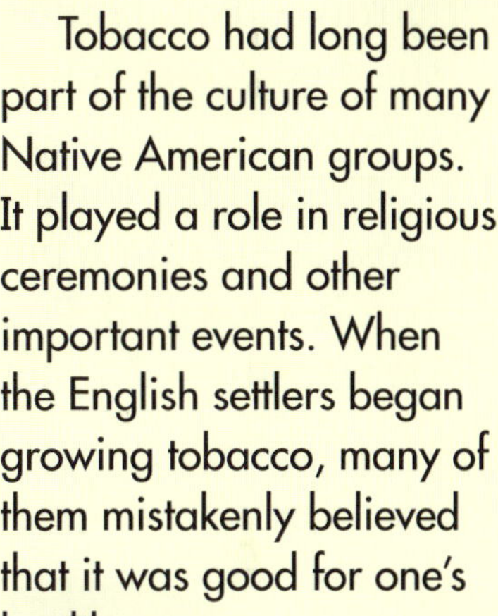

Tobacco, Then and Now

Tobacco had long been part of the culture of many Native American groups. It played a role in religious ceremonies and other important events. When the English settlers began growing tobacco, many of them mistakenly believed that it was good for one's health.

Today, we know that any use of tobacco is harmful to one's health. Tobacco is an addictive drug that can cause cancer and other deadly diseases.

The Deaths of Pocahontas and Chief Powhatan

In 1616, Pocahontas, Rolfe, and their young son, Thomas, sailed to London. Rolfe hoped to convince people in England to give more money to keep Jamestown going strong. He also hoped more settlers would be willing to come to America.

After seven months in England, Rolfe was ready to return to Virginia. However, Pocahontas became too sick to travel. Pocahontas was only about 21 years old when she died. Chief Powhatan had now lost his daughter forever.

Tired of the constant struggles, Powhatan gave up most of his ruling powers. In 1618, about one year after Pocahontas died, Powhatan died.
He was about 70 years old.

The End of Chief Powhatan's World

The flood of English settlers pouring into Virginia proved too powerful even for Powhatan. He hoped that they would unite with his people, but instead they kept going to war.

After Powhatan's death, his younger brother became the new chief. In the years that followed, thousands of the Powhatan people died. Some died in war. Others died from diseases brought over by the English settlers. Forced from their homelands, the Powhatans also suffered from severe food shortages. The struggle between the English and the Powhatan people lasted for decades.

Today, some of the Powhatan people still live on part of their homeland in Virginia. They have survived, passing on their traditions and their long history. They work to keep their culture—and the memory of their great leader, Powhatan—alive as part of the history of all Americans.

Powhatan boy wearing traditional Powhatan clothing

Glossary

authority the power to decide what others may or may not do

ceremony a formal activity conducted for an specific purpose

confederacy groups of people who join together for some common purpose

gentlemen men born of high rank in England who were not used to doing physical work

intervene to come between people to stop a fight or argument

lodge a Native American home

permanent something that lasts

seige encircling and blocking an enemy while attacking them